Untold Sexual Child Abuse Story

Untold Sexual Child Abuse Story

Ijeoma E. Osuji

PARTRIDGE

Print information available on the last page.

To order additional copies of this book, contact
Toll Free 0800 990 914 (South Africa)
+44 20 3014 3997 (outside South Africa)
orders.africa@partridgepublishing.com

www.partridgepublishing.com/africa

TABLE OF CONTENT

DEDICATION

With heart full of joy, I dedicate this book to God Almighty who gave me the knowledge and strength to write.

Thank you my God for seeing me through all my stormy days and bringing me into a fulfilled life.

ACKNOWLEDGMENTS

In life, everyone must have one thing or the other that makes one discover him/herself. So, I honestly thank my husband, Mr. Festus M. Osuji, for helping me discover myself.

I very much acknowledge my lovely lambs for being there for me:

Clinton Chimagoziem, mummy love and bless you, thank you for your love. Divine Angel Chinyeremamaka, I love you my baby for your lovely smiles and songs that keep me going. Sunshine Ugochim, I care a great deal for your true love to me and your smiles, which make me, smile. Praisefull Chibumzor, I am joyful to have you as a true friend, God bless you and Chioma Philomena Osuji, I love and care a great deal for your true love to me and your support. I thank you all my children.

I appreciate you in a special way my younger brother, Uchenna King Didia, for the word of encouragement you always give me and your prayers for me which God had answered, that He (God) had carried me this far. God bless, protect and lead you now and always.Amen.

I appreciate you so much, Mr. Bekee Anyalewechi, the editor-in-chief of The Neigbourhood Newspaper, for all you have been doing for me. You gave me the opportunity to write first in your newspaper and now, in your tight schedule, you made out time to go through this work forwarding it. Thank you very much, sir. God bless you.

I thank you in a special way Chief Gladden Ben-Wakama for making out time to edit this masterpiece. Remain blessed Sir.

Thank you Emmanuel Lucky Eze for helping to type and design this work.

I thank my very good friend, Sabina Onuoha, who stood by me all the time and gave me encouragement to go on; believing that one day this work will surely come to life. You are what a friend should be, I am grateful. God bless you.

FOREWORD

It was my pleasure to go through this humble seminal effort coming from a mother, wife and keen observer. This for sure, is not a fresh page on the issue of sex education, but the angle from which the author opens her brave and bold contributions, deserves commendation.

I made no procrastination in doing that as there are those out there who would prefer to "die in silence." Or, not to be seen as "spoilt ones."

What the author has done through this book is like pulling down the "Berlin Wall." Not only are general instances cited, but the author has revealed what happened to her, as a kid.

From her point of view parents and teachers ought to do the first time teachings on sex education. Failure, whether out of job pressure or other social needs, could be fatal.

Parents and teachers should have this book as daily companion and the practical steps discussed, practiced at home.

BekeeAnyalewechi

INTRODUCTION

In newspapers and magazines, sexual activities are presented in such a manner that the reader feels and sees a live picture in his/her heart. The musicians, actors and actresses are worst, because they display raw sex. My dear, have you ever stopped to ponder the disastrous effect this could have on our young kids and teenagers who are our future hope and leaders of tomorrow? Have you ever felt disturbed about this issue? Have you ever thought of the wrong messages being sent to our lovely and innocent children?

If you have ever thought about these, what do you think the remedy could be? Is it to feign ignorance of the situation, and pose that everything is still in order and like in the past not to educate the children the dangers it posits? It is said that "the right information is power". See Proverbs 14:15: "The unenlightened will believe anything while sensible people watch their steps."

Now, if you will agree with me that as a result of the recent happenings, we ought to educate our kids and teenagers on this global problem and danger, how do we go about it then? When is the right time to start? Since "sex" is a very delicate issue to handle before children.

Notwithstanding, it is a reality in today's world that the effect of its ignorance in children is very devastating. We must brace up as this issue is surely very frightening to many parents, who truly care about their children's welfare. Sex issues are very unpleasant to parents but we should not let the issue of sexual abuse rob us of our happiness and joy. We should rather use our God-given strength and knowledge to protect our kids and teach them what to do at a given time and stage of their lives.

Sex is an issue, which, if left unchecked will lead to premature death amongst teenagers. We preach today to adults and youths of "abstinence from sex" because of HIV/AIDS pandemic, sexually transmitted diseases. Let us not forget that it is very hard to learn the use of the left hand in old age. That is, if we must fight a good war in this regard, we must start very early in life to educate our children about sex, especially on sexual abuse.

We should let the children know the possibility of being abused/molested by some evil people, especially close relatives and neighbours who may claim to render them some help that are rather misguided.

In recent times, there has been controversy among child psychologists as regards the role of parents, teachers and adults in the child's early development. That is, the child's "nature" (what the child has inherited) and "nurture" (the upbringing and training) the child received. Most researchers are convinced that a child's development is influenced by a combination of these two factors: nature versus nurture.

Child-development expert, Dr. J. Frase Mustard explains, "What we clinically now know is that the experience the child is exposed to in the early years of his life influences how that child's brain develops." That is why experts on child sexual abuse advise that we start very early in life (as early as 18 months) to teach a child about sex and sexual abuse.

Sexual abuse is a global problem. In 2006, the then secretary General of the United Nations presented a world report to the UN General Assembly on violence against children compiled by an independent expert. According to the report, an estimated 150 million girls and 75 million boys under 18 years of age experienced forced sexual intercourse or other forms of sexual violence.

Surely those figures are staggering, yet they are certainly underestimate.

A review from 21 countries suggested that in some places as many as 36% of women and 29% of men had been subjected to some form of sexual victimization during childhood. The worst of it is that majority of the perpetrators were relations. As it stands now, these numbers increase by the minute, yet not many have seen any reason to focus on this cancerous phenomenon.

Preachers, Speakers, authors, etc all focus on miracles, financial breakthrough, healing and deliverance. It is mostly these topics that are preached and just very few talk about sex and sexual abuse. Whereas the study of sexual abuse and understanding sex can and will give a child all those liberations being preached.

Not many people today dwell on the subject of child sexual abuse. They shudder at the very thought of it. Such a thing is surely frightening and unpleasant reality in today's world. Its effects on children are always devastating. So the issue is much worth considering. If the fear of sexual abuse is paramount in our heart, what then can we give for the sake of our children's safety?

Learning about the unpleasant realities of abuse is surely a very small price to pay, because such knowledge can really make a difference.

Let us not allow the plague of child sexual abuse rob us of our courage. At least, parents and teachers have the power that our children do not have; strength that will take years and decades, for the children to gain. Old age is often versed with knowledge, experience and wisdom. The most important key there, is to muster those qualities and put them to use in protecting our tender children because:

1. All good and purposeful adults are the child's first line of defense against sexual abuse.

2. Parents and teachers are to give the child some basic education against sexual child abuse as a necessary tool to their growth.

3. And it is the responsibility of parents and teachers to equip the child with some basic protective tools.

In the subsequent chapters, we will be discussing on the above three points outlined but first, the story of how I was abused, how I started this campaign against sexual Child Abuse and my greatest motivation going on these years since 2007 despite not having adequate support will come first.

CHAPTER ONE
MY LIFE STORY

As a child, I suffered a lot of abuses unknown to my parents and it was very hard breaking free.

I was a child of about 6 years when I started knowing about sex but not from my mother or father. It was a girl of about 14 years then, a friend I would say and a close neighbour. She would gather many other children, both boys and girls, from their houses. And will always tell us that she saw one "brother", and "sister" at a place doing "something," that she wants to show us what they were doing and how were they doing it. Then we would ask her what were they doing and how they were doing it? She will then take us to an empty house, lay us down and ask us one after the other to lie on top of her. She will seduce any sex (male or female) she love to use to do her wish at any given time. She does not demonstrate these acts with her age mates but performed these obnoxious acts on younger children who were completely ignorant of the practice. Their house became a common play ground for children and no parent ever cared to find out why.

How she got herself into that I do not know, but I believe a close person must have inculcated such into her. This she continued until we (my family) left that area, hence none of our parents knew what we were doing neither did they think we could do anything of that sought. It told negatively on many of the children whom she used for her misguided practical sex lessons as many were completely lost, especially for those children that were around her. Later, most of them got lost in sex and were consumed by it, in the sense that some due to early knowledge about sex in life could not stop it and got themselves pregnant without getting to JSS 2 and had to drop out of school.

Today, the effect is terrible as it is becoming a global phenomenon. That is what could have been avoided by little vigilance on the part of the parents and stop the abuse being escalated like wild fire. Bear in mind that if you don't teach your child about sexual abuse and sex, many are ready to do so in the way they know best.

The case of a two and half years old girl (ACase Study)

A little girl of about 2 years plus became a target to an abuser and was somehow abused in my neigbourhood sometime 2003. Because I lived with the fearful feeling of abuse in me, I recognized from afar any form of abuse and hated it with all passion. I have always prayed to God to help me educate my future children, friends, well-wishers and neighbours before I reached the age of marriage and got married. The fear of sexual abuse scared me away from both men and women in my adolescent age.

Under the grip of this consciousness, I was always on my own and imagined a lot about sex and the wrong use of it. I was very vigilant and very observant on any child around me, whether a relative or not. I can easily point out abusers/molesters when I see one. When I noticed one, if I cannot talk to him/her, I will quietly find out who the target was and get close to that child whether the child's parents know it or not. I often get close to those supposed victims no matter the age and teach the child little by little what to do to get away quickly before the predator finally strikes. The molester will never know that, that child had knowledge of what to do and will definitely strike, only to find out that the intended victim knows more than he/she thought.

That was what happened in this case. When I noticed that a girl was about to fall a victim, I got acquainted to her by buying her biscuits, ice-cream and many more. Once the parents were out, I assumed their role without anybody questioning my support. Those places I know the abuse will come from, I covered very well. Instead of allowing the molester (in this case of a boy of about 20 years) to bathe the would-be victim, I did it myself in the name that the girl is my little friend so as to protect her from the abuse.

While bathing her, I use the opportunity to tell her that "no one is permitted to touch you in your Virgina expect the way I'm bathing you. If anybody touches you in your Virgina any time, any day, come and tell me or better still tell your mum, okay I told her these words all the time. I also told her to question anybody that touches her in a wrong manner with words like "why are you touching me like that? I will tell my mummy".

I told her that her Virgina is not a "play thing" and she should not allow anyone play with it, no matter who is involved. I told her, I'm not supposed to touch you there except when I am bathing you. Your mummy is not supposed to touch you there except when she wants to clean you up too, likewise your daddy, brother, uncle or anyone. One fateful day, when no one was around, my suspected abuser decided to strike. As I later gathered from the girl, he took her into the bathroom to bathe her and there, abused her. The girl said she tried to stop him with those words I taught her but he shut her up and continued his evil act. The little baby said, "I will tell my mummy" but he thought she was kidding.

When the mother came back, the girl told her mother that "Uncle touched me". The mother made no sense of it. Once the baby saw me, she ran to me and told me, "Aunty, uncle do me." I immediately understood and called her mother's attention to what her daughter was saying. The mother said, "Me I no know, don't mind her she is just being a child or won't someone touch her again"? I said, "Baby, come, where did uncle do you?" The child said, "In my Virgina." I told her mum, why don't you check her first before you conclude that's a child's talk. Then the mother removed the girl's panties and there and then, we saw blood in her body and pants. The mother started crying and behold, people gathered, it was then the mum asked, which Uncle do you this thing? and the child called his name. The uncle was trying to deny but people who saw him enter the bathroom with the girl testified against him.

The boy could not believe that this little girl could act like that. He was more shocked than afraid. The parents of the girl beat him black and blue and called the attention of the police who punished this boy and the rest is history. The parents of the girl and every other person wondered how this girl acquired such knowledge and boldness. When they found out I was the one that taught her, we became friends and they entrusted their children to me without fear, strongly believing their children were in good hands. I felt so happy and thankful to God Almighty for using me to save a soul. This is the genesis of my crusade against sexual child abuse.

The parents also saw the importance of teaching their child, sex and sexual abuse and decided to implement it. The child is now very free from in-house abuse and all forms of sexual abuse. She is bold to speak up for herself and her parents have learnt to make good meaning of children complains.

In every word that comes out from a child, there is an atom of truth. If you don't get it clear, ask questions from the people around to get the whole facts and truth for you.

Some cases gathered from hospitals (Case Study).

1. In this case, the mother was a police officer and the father a driver. Every morning they hurried out of the house leaving their children in the hands of a maid and the younger brother to the father of the house.

When they are gone, the young man of about 23years of age would call the brother's daughter of about 7years of age and say to her, "Let me teach you sex education. This thing I am teaching you, your parents will never teach you and see, it is our secret. You must not tell anyone, for if you do, I will stop teaching you."

Again, he told the little girl that to make sure they keep it very secret; they have to swear an oath to keep the innocent girl from disclosing anything to the parents. So now, he has the girl to himself. Every afternoon, he had sex with this girl in the name of teaching her how the mother and father brought her to the world.

Due to the carelessness of the parents or should I say, over- trust on the part of the parents to the brother in the house, they never found out until this girl started emitting odour due to pus coming out from her vagina as a result of abrasions during intercourse.

It happened one day; the mother had a day off from work and decided to wash her children's clothes. While she was washing, she discovered that her eldest daughter's clothes and pants were stained and smelling. So she called her inside and went close to her and found out that her daughter smelt badly. She closed the door and asked her what the problem was but she refused to say a word.

The mother as a police officer collected her gun and threatened to kill the daughter if she fails to say what was wrong with her. It was then she mentioned the most shocking expose her mother never expected to hear. How the uncle taught her sex education, and how they swore to an oath.

The boy seeing his aunty behind closed doors with her daughter with a hard voice interrogating, sensed what the outcome would be and as such ran for his life. The girl was quickly rushed to the hospital. She spent weeks in the hospital for treatment.

In the second case, the mother and father were civil servants. Every morning, they will rush out as duty calls but before they left each day, they handed over their children to their "good neighbour" to help look after them. The "good neighbour" was a married man, with his family living there. They had shop in front of their house and so, were always around.

Anyone will easily believe that the man being a husband and a father would be least suspected for any form of child sexual abuse but that was not the case. Instead he became a sex teacher to the girl of about 11 years. He bought several gifts for this particular girl who would always have something to discuss with the man, away from others. He made this girl swear an oath.

Oath-taking is a frequently used tactics by molesters/abusers because it scares the children and makes them develop cold feet. Every day the old man had sex with this little girl. For 2 years this went on without anybody finding out. Then, it happened that this girl of about 13 years got pregnant for the "good neighbour".

She never recognized this, neither the man nor the parents for 6 months. She was too young to even know she was pregnant. She was always sick and tired, and could not do much at home, yet the mother or father did not find out. By By the sixth month, the so called "good neighbor" found out and more misguided help was given to the girl that lead to force abortion.

The baby eventually died in the womb. The little girl became severely ill and her parents had to take her to a private hospital where the doctor and nurses quickly made an investigation and discovered what was wrong with her. They asked her who impregnated her but she adamantly refused to open up. They referred them to the General Hospital where they told her parents what the problem was.

The doctors there also told them that the girl's life was in grave danger; (at the point of death). It was then the parents started asking their daughter who the man was but she said nothing to them even when she was dying. She was too annoyed to herself and hated to see her parents for not being adequately cared for. Then her immediate younger brother came and knelt beside his dying sister crying, "Oh my sister, remember how you and I are close to each other. Even if you will not talk to our parents, please my lovely sister, talk to me, who did this to you. For the sake of our love as brother and sister, I beg you in God's name, tell me who this man was and how did it happen. "The dying teenage girl told him who the abuser was but that couldn't save her and she died. Please it is good to note here that it is not the oath that killed the girl; her death was as the result of complications beyond control.

The "good neighbour" on his part, ran away the moment he heard from the parents that doctors said that the girl was pregnant and had tried to abort the baby.

He got the message from the parents who never knew they were talking with the "killer". The same day the girl died, the abuser ran away to avoid the wrath of the parents. He left his family exposing them to danger.

The danger indeed came immediately the girl told the brother everything and died. The angry family rushed home but did not find the so called "good" and "trusted" neighbour at home. They vented their anger on his family members but for other neighbours who ran to the police for quick intervention without which, they would have been killed. (source of the story - true life story).

That is, what the absence of sex education for children could lead to. Irreversible tragedy! Please let us all work to have sex education adopted in to our school curricula for the benefit of all and a healthy society free of sexual child abuse.

Even as we are talking about children with parents, there are children without or guidance. Let the school teach and guide such against sexual child abuse teaching this topic at schools. The later children are more open to sexual child abuse and we all use the same society.

Finally, mothers mostly, let us know:

1. How we dress our young children. Exposing the body of the girl child draws the attention of the abusers.

2. Both parents and teachers should prevent the children from begging and accepting gifts from people, more especially strangers

3. Discourage the child from jumping and hugging adults especially the opposite sex.

4. Giving children cooked food is better to fast food because the later, exposes children to abuse.

All the above instances are true life stories that happen in our country here Nigeria. The below is one from the Internet. Enjoy

Abused!
Draw your conclusion! (My greatest motivation)

After I self published a book on prevention Against Sexual child Abuse 2009.
I found out that getting the book to the public who needs them is not easy. I started sharing the books to everyone close to me. I was invited to television stations and I gave good numbers of the books free which NTA port Harcourt, RSTV etc are among them. Radio houses also invited me on the same topic, prevention of child sexual abuse because of my book.

On my way one day to Saluter from Aggrey Road I entered front seat of a bus and seated beside me was a lady.
I greeted her because she was there before me and older too. But she answered very unfriendly.

I let it be hence I don't know her from Adam. After a little while, I started talking about the child sexual abuse preventive measures to everyone who cares to hear because that was how much I was passionate about getting the message out.

After which i gave out the book each to all in the bus who showed interest. I carry my books around in the quantity i could carry each time.

To my surprise, the lady beside me asked for one, I gave her. She immediately began to talk to me!

I was amazed and most shocked to my root at words coming out of her mouth.

First she requested we spend some time together quietly, I accepted.
We stopped, look for a tree with shade and sat down.

I quote her: "First don't ask me my name for I wont give you. I won't either tell you my house address because I wouldn't want to see you again!

I commend you for this kind of bold step you are taken it's not easy and I am very sure many won't want to help you to continue this campaign but I tell you Madam, never you stop. Go on in every possible way you can and save as many people as you could.

God will be with you.

I will tell you my story, all of it because I will never meet you again. I just listened on without interruption.

She continued, a little bitter smile showed on her face:

"My life is completely destroyed!" You know by who? The people most dear & close to me.

I didn't tell you my name in case if I am still here on earth when you will write about me, I won't hear my name either as friction or real.

She said, it is not enough that you have done this, do more. Write on how to teach children in schools starting from nursery and make it part of school books. So that children whom there abuse will learn from schools how to protect themselves from such evil and also know how to get away quickly and seek help.

Hummm! My sister what am telling you is not an easy task but you must continue and always learn new ways to do this work.

Truly, I was getting real scaled but I maintained. I was imagining how on earth I would do what she was telling me but I accepted all the same.

She then began: Madam, your name is Ijeoma. Yes madam Ijeoma, and my life was ruined.

It started when I was young. My mother left my father and remarried. I was left staying with my father. He won't let me alone with anyone. He buys me gifts more than I can use. He does not allow me watch movies alone until that 8years of my life she said.

Tears rolling down a now full grown woman's eyes and I too couldn't control my own tears due to emotional pains I am experiencing because of her ugly story.

She continued, at 8years I have somehow known that what father is doing with me is wrong. That made me become very wild and uncontrollable because my father don't have mouth where I am anymore.

Then an uncle came to stay with us and did the same. He takes me to party and fun places made for adults. I thought I was enjoying my life not knowing I was allowing those wicked men to destroy me. I don't know how to say no to any man that request. Before the age of 10years, I have run out of the house many times.

Then, I decided to go stay with my mother and her husband and that was another mistake. As the step father did not spare me either. When I complained to my mother, she was so annoyed with me. She called me all manner of names.

I then decided never to speak to anyone ever again of the things happening in my life. I slept with many men just at request which the majority is close relations.

Till now I am not married. My son is also growing up in the street as myself. I don't have control over my life.

Bitter experiences that happened in my early life still controls me no matter how hard I tried.

Many in hotels as prostitutes are from wealthy families like me, went to good schools but was destroyed by their own closest supposed loved ones.

If there is a subject in school that covers this then, my life would have had a different turn!

Now you see why I asked you from the onset that you should make promise to write how to teach children and take it to schools.

By the end of her story, my clothes were soaked with tears.
I was speechless, heartbroken and truly afraid!

I reassured her that I don't know how I will do it but I must write on how to teach children and also take it to schools.

This happened 2009.

2012, I published "Total guide on prevention to child sexual abuse" and I also took them to ministry of Education Rivers State and it got approved for junior secondary schools but its yet to be used round the schools.
Part of my promise fulfilled and "never drop it" is still there.
This woman whom I don't know who she is, weather alive or dead is one of my strongest motivation.
As she said that it won't be easy, it isn't easy at all.
But I give all glory to God who has taken me thus far.

CHAPTER TWO

PARENTS AS CONTRIBUTORS TO CHILD SEXUAL ABUSE

Parents can also abuse their child by themselves. When husband and wife romance each other in the presence of their children, they are in effect, exploring the child natural curiosity about sex and making the child arouse to wanting to do same. Same way children feel hurt when they see their parents argue or fight. is the same way they feel arouse when they see their parent in an uncompromising state.

Case Study: Aparticular family known to me

There is a particular family known to me. The husband and wife will always kiss, romance and hold each other anywhere and anytime, even in the presence of their children, and even lie together not minding. Maybe to them, their children will not border because they are their parents. They call each other all the romantic names ever known.

You know what? It caused the children to start early in life to romancing boys of their age openly with no fear or shame. If one tried to caution them, they simply say, "It is not bad" because our parents do it always without shame. The resultant effect is that the two daughters of this couple got pregnant while in secondary school.

Before the parents could realize their mistakes, the deed had been done. It caused their father heart attack and he died. Out of ignorance, he failed in his duties both to God and mankind.

The lesson in this reference is that caution should be taken while playing the game so as not to corrupt the children. Parents should display show of love, honesty, care and discipline before their children, so that they (children) will learn these good acts and qualities from them and exhibit same to transform the society for better.

Another source of corrupting the children, is by playing the act why sleeping together with their children in the same room, thinking that their kids are asleep.

This one is very common with many parents especially those families that share one room or two rooms. It is neither the parents making nor the children but a common fate that befell such homes. Therefore, in such situation, parents have to be very careful and conscious of themselves for the sake of the children. Many surveys carried out have proven that such situation had put many children in the act of incest in the house, while they are still young. Incest is forbidden in the Bible and carries a great curse too. It is where brother and sister from the same womb have sex or father and daughter have sex or even mother and son sleep together.

This situation has caused many family unbearable pains.

Some of the parents found out but very late and only through the pregnancy of their daughters. Some other parents never find out but share the shame and curse such evil act had hipped on them.

No one watches a pornography picture or magazine without a strong urge to practice it. So when children watch their parents in the act of having sex whether we admit it or not, the children are bound to experiment same. Of a truth; children believe parents and teachers to be perfect all the time. They learn from their parents and teachers most traits, whether good or bad. That is why it is advised for teachers to model characters and parents who find themselves in a tight situation should try and sacrifice time for their children. It shows a high mark of discipline.

In a further development as the story goes around the neighborhood, the father, mother, a boy and a girl live in a single room apartment. From the source of the story, it's the practice of the parents to always make love in the night when they believe their children would be in deep sleep. One night, the husband made a request but the wife refused saying "this children could be awake". The husband insisted but his wife adamantly refused and a little misunderstanding ensued. Then surprisingly, their son intruded "please you people should do whatever you want to do and leave us alone to sleep, when did you start to border about our presence?" What does such statement imply? This act would not only introduce the children to sex but many other bad acts. If they can not practice what they've learnt from the parents at home, they would and could go out in search of other places to satisfy their overwhelming urge.

The regrettable thing here is that parents do not teach their children about sex and pretends that everything is okay even after exposing their children to early sex and abuse. To parents, they believe, the children will understand. What will they understand? Who is expected to understand the other on this issue? If you are a parent that finds yourself in a situation like this and desires to make amends, a lot could be done to improve your "state" and that of the child that had suffered abuse in your hands. Call to get directories of counselors who can help you.

There are two things sexual abuse exposes children to. Any child that has suffered abuse must have either of them. They are; (1) The child becomes wayward in every aspect of it. (2)

The child withdraws from people of both sex and other social activities. None is good. It takes the grace of God to bring them out from any of these vices.

My book, on Total Guide on Prevention Against Child Sexual Abuse provides the needed ingredients in educating children on sex and sexual abuse from tender age of 18 months and above.

CHAPTER THREE

PATTERN OF SEDUCTION TO CHILD ABUSE

Abusers are very clever in this unholy act and do not use force on their victims. Most are well known by their victims and probably respected and welcomed by their victims. With the knowledge that their victims know nothing about sex education, they begin their seduction gradually.

An abuser begins by selecting a target. A target here means a child who appears vulnerable, a novice in sex education; the one relatively easy to seduce. Next, he singles out that child for special attention. He then tries to win the trust of the child's parents, in order that he will have the opportunity to spend time privately with the child.

Molesters and abusers are always experts at pretense. They feign sincere interest in the child and family, just to get what they want.

The next step, the abuser begins grooming the child for the act. He gradually becomes physical with the child through unsuspected display of affection, playing, wrestling and tickling the child always. He may also give gifts to the child and when the parents protest, he (abuser) will simply say to them, "The child is worth it". Then, gently he begins to single out the child and separate him/her from friends, siblings and parents. At this point, the abuser will instruct the child to keep secret some gifts or plans for their future excursion from the parents. When he (molester) has won the child's trust, and that of the parents, his tactics has paid off. What then follows is the seduction stage in which the predator is ready to make his moves anytime and anywhere he wants.

Another is that, he is very gentle about it rather than violent or forceful, to avoid the child suspecting anything. He may exploit the child's natural curiosity about sex that is offering to act as a "sex teacher" to the child, since; the child has no education on sex from the parents. He will say to the child, "your parents will never teach you what I am teaching you, so don't I have your respect and trust for this?" Some will tell the child that they play a "special game" together that only both of them will know about.

The abuser goes further to expose the child to pornography in order to make sure the behaviour seems normal and okay.

When the abuser has finally gotten the child, he is now very eager to ensure that the child does not tell anyone of his/her deadly acts. He will use many tactics like threats, blackmail, blame, oath or combination of all to make sure his act remains a secret. For example, he will say to the child, "It is your fault for what happened. Don't ever say it or your parents will see you as a bad child".

The abuser may go further to threaten the child that the oath administered will kill him/her. Or he will say, "Remember it is our secret, if you talk, I will deny you and no one will believe you. They will only say it is a child's talk and thereby lay the whole blame on you". Some will even say, "If your parents ever find out, I will kill your parents and you too".

Child abusers and molesters have no end to the malicious tactics they use to get children, to keep their mouths shut. Therefore, it is in your hands to pay close attention to your child and make the child a difficult target for molesters and abuser.

It is important from time to time to know if the child is going through mental torture or not by making meaningful reasons into some of those "careless" utterances from the child and acting on it. This societal enigma is around us, with us and within us.

Many home movies have shown the devastation sexual abuse has done in the family when left unchecked and where parents have no time for children due to work and as such did not educate the children on this issue. Parents and teachers jointly, should fight a good war in this subject matter and get desired results. Let us all work towards it. It is achievable.

CHAPTER FOUR

PARENTS/TEACHER:
AS FIRST LINE DEFENSE AGAINST SEXUAL CHILD ABUSE

In the past, the word "sex' was scarcely mentioned in public, even among elders, let alone in the midst of children. Sex was highly respected and was kept a secret from children. No parent ever thought of discussing issues relating to sex in the presence of the children, but since after the Enlightenment centuries (18 and 19), this idea was changed and the reverse is now the case. The issue of sex and human sexuality are now discussed in public with every delight.

Sex is no more hidden as it has become the hottest business to sell. Musicians, actors and actresses, the media houses- radio and TV stations, newspapers and magazines use sex related stories and pictures to facilitate increased sales. Anyone that does not include show of sex in his/her business no longer sells. Many marketers now use very beautiful girls as their means of attraction to their productions.

One could easily see naked boys and girls dancing on the road in the name of entertainment and means of livelihood. What a great change! The once "hidden act" is now "an open secret". What is our fate? What is the fate of the children who see what they do not understand or know not how to handle? Most media houses transmit sex on air regardless of who is watching. They are therefore, the large scale contributors to unguided sex and sex abuse affecting our children.

The primary responsibility for protecting children against abuse is in the hands of the parents and teachers. Education is not only the ability to read and write, it is the ability to act upon what has been read. Here are few things you need to know about child abuse:

1. You need to know who abuses children and how he/she goes about it. Parents always think that molesters are strangers lurking in the shadows seeking ways to kidnap, molest or rape their children. They forgot that the people involved in this dastardly act are mostly relatives and neighbours.

Though strange molesters certainly do exist but they are relatively rare. It is instructive to note that about 80% of child sexual abuse, the perpetrator is someone known very well to the child. Someone the child trusts as relatives or neighbours. Ordinarily, one would not believe that a brother or sister, neighbour, teacher, healthcare worker, coach or even a trader close to you could do this act. But in most cases, researches have come to a conclusion that they are the ravening wolves. Nevertheless, you have to be cautious not to be suspicious of everybody around you. Yet you must be very careful and act with wisdom towards protecting the children against sexual abuse. It is good to find out how molesters operate, knowing those tactics can equip the parents and teachers better, and well-prepared to act as the first line of defense.

For example, if someone appears to be very interested in your child in a suspicious manner by giving special attention to your child, giving expensive gifts to the child, or offers free babysitting or private excursion, you have to keep a very close watch.

Monitor every movement of the person but unknown to him/her. While keeping a close watch, do not jump to conclusion because some times, such person may be innocent. However, as your child's first line of defense, you must be on the alert. The Bible says, "Anyone inexperienced puts faith in every word, but the shrewd ones considers his steps."

Remember, any offer that sounds too good to be true may just be scrutinized. So carefully watch anyone who volunteers to spend time alone with your child. Let such an individual know that you are likely to check on your child any time and any minute and such vigilance may sound extreme, but you rather be safe than sorry.

Be actively involved in your child's activities, friendship and schoolwork; make out quality time for your children

Both parents should not be involved in career jobs at the same time. Know that the world is full of evil, so sacrifice your time for the sake of your children, till they can stand on their own. In this way, God who has put these children under your charge will be happy with you. Remember, there are those still looking for the fruit of the womb.

It will be right for parents to come into agreement of how their children should be taken care of in their absence. It is pertinent that the most capable hand work for the family while the others do some trade or skills to assist the family and at the same time be homely with the children. "I love my kids", as we all say, do not show true love. But our bid to bring them uprightly is the true love. We suffer for the children, but most times, they don't appreciate it because they feel neglected the way we leave them and go to work. So, for the love of your children, try to spend quality time with them. For spending time with children pleases them more than anything or any gift we could think of.

A mental health professional who spent 33 years working on cases of sexual abuse noted that he has seen countless cases that could have been prevented by simple vigilance on the parents'/ teachers' part because sexual child abuse happens both at school and home. The mental health professional quoted one convict saying: "Parents literally give up their children. They surely made it easy for me". This in effect calls to mind that, most molesters prefer easy targets.

Parents who are actively involved in their children's affairs and lives make their children very difficult targets. Always listen to your children very well and make out good meaning of their words. Children rarely disclose abuse or the likes directly. They are ashamed, worried and afraid of the outcome. But when a child says, "Mum, I do not want that person or babysitter again" promptly ask why? If he/she says that an adult played funny games with him/her, ask, what kind of game? If a child says someone tickled me, ask "where?"

Please, parents, teachers and all that care about the welfare of the child, do not be quick to dismiss children's talks and answers because abusers do threaten them that "No one will believe you" and that is true in most cases.

It is good for us to support a child that has been molested to recover because such support is a very big step to outliving the experience and forge ahead.

The support to an abused child comes through seminars, psychotherapy and healthy children's get-together that gives them opportunity to discover who they are.

My advice to parents, teachers, school authorities and every concerned citizen about child sexual abuse is to support the awareness and seminars on this issue.

QUESTIONS:

1. To effectively be the first line of defense against sexual child abuse, parents/teachers and children themselves should find out who the abusers are and the way they operate. ***True/False.***

   (b) Write short note to support your answer.

2. Do a survey in the class to find out how children will support their parents work all day without sharing time with them.

3. I love my kids as we all say, does not show true love but our bid to bring them uprightly shows true love. ***Propose/Oppose the above statement.***

4. The mental health professional quoted one convict saying "Parents literally give up their children. They surely made it easy for me". ***True/False.***

5. Which children are hard target to abusers?

CHAPTER FIVE

BASIC BACKGROUND EDUCATION ON SEXUAL ABUSE

One reference work on the subject of child abuse quotes a convicted molester as saying, "Give me a kid who knows nothing about sex, and you've given me my next victim" These words are very useful reminder to parents.

Children who are ignorant about sex are much easier for molesters to fool. The Bible says that knowledge and wisdom can deliver us "from the man speaking perverse thing" (Proverbs 2:10-12). Is this not what we want for our children? If it is, then, it is not right to withhold the teaching of sex and sexual abuse of the child from our homes and schools. For it is better thought to our children by ourselves so as to give the right teaching to avoid abuse.

The girl (Amina) I helped during my IT at Amaraku, Imo State in 2002 could serve as a case study for teaching every child on sex and prevention. Below is the story.

1. During my Industrial Training Exercise at Amaraku in 2002, There is this pretty girl, Amina I met. She was 11 years old. I quietly but closely monitored her and found out that she enjoyed "funny" plays, to be realistic she indulged in sex with her mates around the neighbourhood.

When I found out this, I was not happy. I then asked myself should I inform her parents or exercise a friendly approach with a deliberate intention to prevent her from corrupting other children and at the same time damaging her life. Then I contemplated within myself that if I have the hope of educating my own children on those issues in time to come, then this is an opportunity for me. With humility and tenderness, I began to educate her with the believe that her parents have little or no knowledge of the subject matter.

So it was dawn on me to start this crusade with this little girl, Amina who was not my sister or child. I started by drawing her close to myself, accepting her as my little friend, giving her moral education and little gifts that children love. That made her to see me as a good friend and whom to trust. Then I took the next step by discussing with her issues like "men are very tricky and clever in taking away our virginity". This includes me. She felt very free to talk to me and asked questions where necessary. One day she asked me, "Aunty, what is virginity?"

By those discussions, but unknown to her, learning had started. I explained to her that virginity means purity, spotlessness and most especially preserving oneself from having sex till marriage. I told her that virginity in the Bible is a very precious thing to treasure and that is in her hands to make herself a pride and sought-after.

I explained to her that she is a pretty girl and that she should be careful not to fall an easy prey to girls predators. I also emphasized that any man or boy that approaches her on the road, telling her that she is beautiful, elegant and all that bluff", that she should remind them it is the Lord's doing and that she is aware of that. Then a bomb shell to follow; anything else for you to say? Tell him; "look at yourself telling a small girl, you are pretty so that you can molest me. "My dear, I keep my beauty for God who made me and for myself". At that point, she should leave the person alone and walk away.

One day, she came back to tell me, "Aunty, do you know that what you told me was true. As I was coming back from the market, a boy just intercepted my way and I stopped, only for him to praise me, girl, you are very beautiful. I love you, will you be my lover?" And what did you say?" I asked looking for an expected negative reaction and she said, I told him I know I am beautiful but that is for God and me.

You want to defy me, to see a girl of my age and telling her that. At this point, she said that the boy reacted angrily and said Oh! Who has impacted on this girl this kind of knowledge and wisdom?" She left him and came back to the house. I was happy that she was able to act-out the way I taught her. We have to direct our children repeatedly till they can stand on their own. The parents of the girl never knew what transpired between me and their daughter, neither did they know that their daughter had any experience about sex then.

2. It is also important that you should start early in life to name all the parts of the body for the child without withholding the private parts. Some parents will tell their children that penis is "mntata" what that means I do not know. My five year old boy, knew from me that his penis was private, personal and not a toy to play with, when he was under two. It's not for mummy, not for daddy, not even for your aunty or a doctor to play with.

It is your own I told him and if I your mum wants to bath you there, I am to take permission from you just to clean you up, likewise any other person. I told him these words always to make sure he does not forget. I also assured him to come and tell me if anybody touches him in a wrong manner at his penis regardless of who is involved.

Experts in child care and abuse recommend that all parents should have similar talks with their children. In today's world, children need to know that there are people who want to touch them in areas that are wrong both in the sight of man and God.

These warnings need not to instill into children fear or make them distrust all adults. No, it is just one safe message among many others. Most of them know nothing about abuse and you don't paint it in a way that will put fear into the child but in a way that he/she enjoys it and eventually uses the message for its purpose. It has not created in my son any fear but has exposed him to the issues early enough in life.

Children love playing and not forceful action like, commanding a child to sit and learn when he/she wants to play.

Therefore, teach them as if they are playing, yet emphasize your points and let them understand it. That is, at any time; chip in words that are meaningful and good to their heart. Children learn fast and anything you inculcate in them remains in them (Prov. 22:6)

As we know, a child's education includes learning to obey, because teaching a child to obey is very important, yet a very difficult lesson.

All the same, such lessons can go too far and if a child is taught that he must always obey any adult, regardless the circumstances, he is open to abuse because molesters are quick to notice when a child is overly compliant. Most parents teach their children that obedience is relative. *The relative here means that a child should not obey what he/she knows that is wrong just because it is coming from an Elder or a known relative.* For Christian parents, it is not as complicated as it sounds because this simply means telling children not to accept anything that is contrary to God's word. Even Mummy and Daddy should never tell you to do something God says its not good and as such evil.

*Very importantly, children should always inform their parents, if anyone tries to get them to do something wrong or something they don't understand.

3. Another and very important point is to let the child know that anything someone asks him/her to keep secret from you (their parents and teachers) is wrong. The child should immediately inform the parents or the teachers as the case may be. It is good to make them know that such a person does not mean well for them, no matter who he/she is, should not be trusted.

Make them also know that it is always good to tell their parents what they do, say or see. It is always good to assure children to love God, say the truth regardless of what happened, and obey right, that is to obey what God Almighty permits and be firm to say "No!" to what is wrong and degrading in the sight of God. Even when a child does something that is wrong, no matter how bad, it is very good and okay to always go to the Mum or Dad to tell them about it all. The child should be made to know that. Let us make our children our best friends and our children will obey us and God with ease.

In conclusion, let us plan to educate our children early enough and prepare them against possible misguided information by the predators that may not be needed by the child. Let us be at alert because we are living in a world where selfishness rules the heart of many.

QUESTIONS:

1. Explain how you can use the basic protective tools.

2. It is good to start early to name all the parts of the body of the child without withholding the private parts? *If YES Support and If NO support.*

3. Is it good for a child to keep secret from the parents/teachers?

CHAPTER SIX

EQUIPPING THE CHILD AGAINST SEX PREDATORS ON THE PROWL WITH BASIC PROTECTIVE TOOLS

In this chapter, we try to equipt the child with precautionary measures in case someone tries to take advantage when parents/guidance are not around to monitor. A method that is often recommended is like a game, thus, parents or teachers should put questions that are unexpected to test the intelligence and awareness of that child. Such questions could go in the following pattern. Example, what if...? What about....? and hear the child answer it. Parents or teachers can generate a story to make the children understand better.

Case Study One - MentalAlertness

Putting this story to the child thus; we went out and robbers came to the house, you, the child had access to escape, what will you do?" His/her answer might not be what you expect but you will hear his/her answer, and then judge his/her intelligence. Then guide the child mildly on the right way you want.

Parents/teachers should teach the child on how to be firm and rigid in saying "NO" to abusers and molesters, like "Stop it", Don't do that", "No, I said, I don't want that," and many more protective words and ways to act them. These words put off any child abuser completely and put fear in them (abusers). Parents and guidance, especially mothers and teachers, should make themselves available and creative in order to help and train up children in the best possible ways.

Case Study Two - Emotional Development

You can create a story for a child to spice up his/her emotions in line with an expected situation bearing in mind that children learn by playing and imitation.

Taking for instance, Oge was dropped by her mother at her aunty's place to stay while her mother attends a function. Do you know that Oge's aunty whom Oge and her mother trusted very well was not who they believed her to be. No sooner Oge's mother left, than the aunty started caressing

Oge. Instead of Oge being tantalized reacted negatively and shouted at her, "stop it," "I don't like it," "I will tell my mum. The Aunty was shocked and felt very much ashamed and left her alone".

Such stories would send a good message into the child. "Tell me my love, what will you do if you were the one? Will you act wisely as a child of God and do as Oge did, by shunning the person?" From the above simple and little story, you have taught the child what to do, and no matter how dull the child is, he/she will give you the exact answer you expect. This is teaching a child with basic protective tools. An author says that "A firm No!" or "don't do that!" and "leave me alone!" does wonders to frighten the seductive offender into retreat and into rethinking his/her choice of victim.

Let us help our children act out brief scenarios so that they feels confident to refuse loudly, get away quickly and be able to report to us whatever that may have happened. Again, a child who seems to understand the training thoroughly may easily forget it within a few weeks or months, so there is need to repeat this training regularly.

All child care givers, including the fathers, step fathers, brothers, uncles and every male relative should be part of these discussions and training because all involved in this teaching are in effect, promising the child that they will never commit such atrocity. More so, these are mostly the anticipated molesters. It is very sad to say that much sexual abuse occurs right within the confines of the family.

In summary, in giving the basic protective tool, every adult should bring his or her wisdom in creating stories for children that will help them be at alert and act accordingly when confronted with the issue. All concerned should help the child get enough awareness, either in form of seminar, books or handouts

Every adult should help to instill boldness and confidence on the child for those qualities scares away child molesters.

Most importantly, mothers do not let a boy or any man bath your girl child. Be it the father or any close male relative. Also do not let any housemaid, any girl or any woman birth your son especially from the age of nine (9) years.

This above scenario encourages sexual child abuse very much.

QUESTIONS:

1. If there is a robbery attack in the house, you the child escaped. Will you run to a neighbours house to hide or run to close-by police station for help to rescue your family?

2. The girl Oge in this chapter is a brave, obedient and confident child. *True/False?*

3. Is it good for a boy or man to bath a baby girl? *If YES, support and if NO, support.*

CHAPTER SEVEN
SOME WORDS CHILDREN SHOULD KNOW MEANINGS RELATING TO SEXUAL ABUSE

1. **Virginity:** This means pure and spotless. One who has no knowledge of sex in any manner, or one who preserves his or herself till marriage.

2. **Wayward:** One difficult to control especially his/her sexual desires.

3. **Incest:** Sex between a brother and sister from the same womb, a mother and son or a father and daughter.

4. **Homosexual:** A boy or man sexually attracted to his fellow boy or man. Or a man who has sex with his fellow man.

5. **Lesbian:** A girl or woman sexually attracted to her fellow girl or woman. Or a woman or girl who has sex with her fellow woman.

6. **Homophobia:** One who strongly dislikes and fear homosexual.

7. **Rape:** To force one to have sex with you when the person does not want to, by threatening the person with harmful objects, exploring the person's natural curiosity of sex in the case of a child or using violence.

8. **Rapist:** One who forces someone to have sex when the person does not want to.

9. **Sex:** The state of intercourse between a male and a female or the act of a man and woman sleeping together.

10. **Sex Maniac:** One who loves to have sex all the time and has it more often than normal.

11. **Sex Object:** One known only for sex and is not good for any other thing. Not good in character or intelligence.

12. **Sexual Harassment:** This means advances made to someone either by physical contract or comments about sex that the person being spoken to finds annoying and offensive, usually at

school between a teacher and student, at home between a father and an housemaid, in-laws or family friends, at work between a boss and staff.

Some other facts we are expected to let our children know are.

1. There is nothing wrong with sex. If you do not "use" wisely and at the right time, it will only produce pains and load of guilt. But if "used" rightly and at the right time, it brings happiness and joy.

2. It is very necessary to know that it is not important to have sex. One can live a normal life without sex

3. God does not kill anyone if you do not have sex; instead God kills if you abuse sex

4. You as a child, teenager or youth need to fulfill your destiny in life. To do that, you need emotional commitment and sex is emotional and done by the heart. The same thing with fulfilling your destiny in life, you cannot do two emotional things at same time, one must come first.

5. Sex is not love at all but abuse of love among children and teenagers. It can cloud one's reasoning thereby making the most brilliant, the dullest, the most loved, the most hated.

6. What one believes about sex will determine how one behaves and what becomes of the person of it.

7. Lastly, sex to me is a covenant exchange of life, love and pleasure between a man and woman in the right environment for the purpose of peace and happiness for mature minds.

Try to paint a clear picture of pain, pleasure and love in your mind as regard to sex and see where sex falls after indulging in it outside wedlock.

One of my poems called "friend" that has featured in The Neigbourhood Newspaper has the definition of what I believe a child, teenager or youth needs to know and be in relationship till marriage, in other to get his/herself discovered. And my inspiring corner in Education Rescuer could help and give children and teenagers aims/objectives in life and means to achieve them. It runs monthly.

Two of my unpublished books, "A great you" and "My Leadership empire" specially written for children and teenagers in the simplest language will bring out the greatness in any child who reads it and also build an everlasting empire for such children. **www.facebook.com/ijeoma e osuji**

GLOSSARY
(in alphabetical orders according to chapters)

IMPORTANT NOTE:

WORD	MEANING
Abstinence:	Not doing something or staying away from something
Abused:	Use something wrongly or treating people wrongly
According:	following instruction in order
Appreciate:	Be thankful or saying thank you
Centuries:	100 years
Companion:	Somebody that spend more time with you
Complied:	Do something as you are told to do it
Contribution:	Doing your part or effort
Controversy:	Disagreement, different opinions
Convinced:	Cause to Agree
Delicate:	Easily broken
Deserves:	Qualify to receive a gift or something
Devastating:	Destroying
Disastrous:	Causing great danger
Disturbed:	Making somebody restless not having peace of mind.
Effect:	Make happen or bring about
Enlightenment:	Give understanding or make people to understand
Entertained:	Provide Enjoyment and make people laugh and happy
Estimate:	The amount, the important of a thing
Experienced:	Knowledge you gained for a very long time
Expert:	A person that have special knowledge
Feign:	Pretend
Frightened:	Cause to be afraid
Global:	The whole world or worldwide
Ignorance:	Lacking knowledge or not knowing
Independent:	Free from Control
Intercourse:	A man and woman having Sex.
Liberation:	Set free

Majority:	Great number or people.
Misguided:	Showing bad way or direction
Molest:	Force somebody to have Sex.
Muster:	Bring people together or be encourage.
Nature:	Physical things God made
Nurture:	Bring Up
Observer:	Notice or watch carefully
Paramount:	Top or most important
Pandemic:	Disease the whole world have or experiencing
Perpetrators:	People carrying out bad action or supporting bad thing
Plaque:	Disease, curse or affliction
Pleasure:	Enjoyment or satisfaction
Ponder:	Consider or think about
Procrastination:	Delay or postpone action
Prowl:	Move in a restless way
Rearing:	Bring up & care for Children
Regardless:	Show no Concern
Relevant:	Important, applicable or related
Remedy:	Medicine, treatment or cure
Render:	Provide services or help
Researchers:	People that study and lean to know new things.
Reverse:	Move back ward or turn to the other side
Scarcely:	Not common or every where
Seminar:	Tutorial, discussion group or class
Shudder:	To shake, afraid or cold to think something is not good
Situation:	Position or condition of something
Staggering:	Walking without a balance
Transmit:	Passing message or a thing from one person to another
Unchecked:	Something harmful, not been controlled or stopped from getting worse
Underestimate:	Think or guess that the amount of something, size or cost is smaller than it really is
Victimization:	Make somebody suffer unfairly because you are bigger or stronger
Violence:	Harsh behaviour that is intended to hurt or kill
Welfare:	General health, happiness and safety of a person

CHAPTER ONE

Baby Sitting:	Take care or look after a child while the parents are not around
Conclusion:	Final decision about something or somebody

Defense:	Act of protecting somebody or something from attack
Excursion:	A short journey made for pleasure either between two or more people
Expenses:	Costing a lot
Frequently:	Happening or doing something often
Individual:	Person or considered separately
Instructive:	Giving a lot of useful information
Lurking:	Waiting somewhere secretly, especially because you are going to do something bad or illegal
Monitor:	Check that something is done fairly and honestly
Ordinarily:	Says what happened before, saying that it is not happening now or again.
Prepared:	Ready and able to deal with something.
Professional:	Special training or skill
Promptly:	Without delay
Rare:	Existing only in small numbers and therefore valuable and interesting.
Scrutinized:	Look at or examine something very carefully.
Seeking:	Looking for or trying to get something mentioned
Shadows:	Hidden place or something you can not easily see
Stranger:	A person you do not know.
Suspicious:	Feeling that somebody has done something wrong, illegal or dishonest without having any proof.
Tactics:	Method or way one use to achieve something
Tricks:	Make somebody believe something which is not true
Volunteers:	Person who does a job without being paid for
Wolves:	Wild animal of the dog's family. A person who looks friendly, harmless but is really an enemy

CHAPTER TWO

Alert:	Able to think quickly or quick to action
Assure:	To tell somebody something is definitely true or going to happen especially, when they are not sure of it
Circumstance:	Conditions and facts that are connected with and affect a situation
Complicated:	Hard to understand
Continuously:	Something going on without stopping
Convicted:	Found guilt
Corrupting:	Bad effect on somebody or something
Damaging:	Having a bad effect on somebody or something
Defy:	Disobey or useless something
Degrading:	Treating somebody without value

Difficult:	Not easy to control
Discussing:	Talking about somebody or something.
Emphasize:	Value something or somebody by speech or writing.
Escape:	Move away from danger or where you are not allowed to move away
Eventually:	At last or serves in event
Exposed:	Uncovered or out in the open
Forcefully:	Against your will
Funny:	Making you laugh or relaxed
Furious:	Very angry
Further:	Going on
Impact:	Teach
Indulged:	Do something you love, mostly seen as a bad thing
Intercepted:	Cover someone's way or stop one from trying to move.
Involved:	Take part in something.
Issues:	Topic to talk about, mostly important
Marriage:	Legal relationship between husband and wife
Obedience:	Unquestioning action.
Permits:	Allow somebody to do something or allow something happen
Planned:	Actions well known before doing
Precious:	Special and worth a lot of money
Probably:	Used to say that something is true.
Purpose:	Aim, intention, plan, point or ideal
Quotes:	Repeat the same word another person said.
Realistic:	Tell the truth as it is
Recommends:	Tell somebody that something is good and useful
Reference:	Mention somebody or something else
Regardless:	Paying no attention.
Reminder:	Something that makes you remember someone or something
Route:	Area or way.
Similar:	Look alike
Sought-after:	Wanted or needed by many people because it is very good.
Spotlessness:	Perfectly clean, immaculate white.
Surprised:	Shock, astonished and unaware
Tenderness:	Gently and softly
Transpired:	Happened
Treasure:	Valuable such as silver gold or diamond
Victim:	Attacked, injured or killed as a result of crime.
Virginity:	One who never have sex before.
Withhold:	Not to say or give away something

CHAPTER THREE

Atrocity:	Forbidden
Brief:	Short
Commandment:	Laws or Rules
Commit:	Do something wrong like murder or abuse a child
Confident:	Happy about yourself and the things you can do
Confines:	Jail, detain and lock up
Emotions:	Feeling e.g. anger and love are strong emotions
Exact:	Completely correct
Family:	Group of people related to each other
Firmly:	Strong control or grip hold
Frighten:	Make someone afraid
Happened:	Done or occurred
Intelligence:	Ability to learn and understand things
Judge:	Opinion about something after you have thought carefully.
Loudly:	Openly or in a loud way
Mildly:	Gentle, not hot or strong.
Occurs:	Happens
Offenders:	Someone who commits a crime
Quickly:	Fast or at once.
Refuse:	Saying no
Regularly:	Always
Repeat:	Do it again and again
Rigid:	Not easy to change or bend
Scenarios:	Imagine how things could happen
Seductive:	Attracts in a way that want you to do it.
Shocked:	Feel surprised and upset
Spice:	Give a good taste to something
Taught:	Teach
Thoroughly:	Completely, total careful
Training:	Special activity in which you learn how to do a particular job or play a sport.
Unexpectedly	Something you did not believe or know it will happen
Victim:	Attacked, made ill, robbed or killed
Wonders:	Thinks about something and try to give a solution or bring out the truth.

CHAPTER FOUR

Feeling:	Ability to feel.
Forbidden:	Banned, not allowed or illegal
Gathered:	Come or bring together
Hardship:	Poverty, Lack or Need
Honestly:	Truth
Hurt:	Harm or kill
Ignorance:	Lack knowledge
Imply:	Meaning
Introduce:	Bring in, launch or begin
Lay:	Put down, arrange or position
Mistake:	Wrong choice
Misunderstood:	Fail to understand correctly
Mark:	Spot
Overwhelming:	Great

CHAPTER FIVE

Abound:	Grow, do well, boom or increase
Adamantly:	Stubbornly
Apartment:	Dwelling or Public Housing
Arouse:	Stir up
Assumed:	Unspecified
Attack:	Hit, assault or molest
Avoid:	Shun, keep away from
Bear:	Stand or put up with
Border:	Boundary, limit or edge
Common:	Ordinary or everyday
Completely:	Totally or finally
Conscious:	Mindful, alert or aware
Consume:	Eat, drink or devour
Covered:	Sheltered
Curiosity:	Interest, nosiness or prying
Deed:	Act or action
Definitely:	Certainly or truly
Demonstrate:	Show, exhibit or express
Discipline:	Orderly
Educate:	Teach, instruct or train
Effect:	Result

Ensure:	Make sure or guarantee
Exploring:	Discover, look at or search
Exposed:	Reveal or public notice
Fearful:	Scared, afraid or terrified
Inculcate:	Instill or impact
Observant:	Alert, watchful or vigilant
Obnoxious:	Hateful, horrible or unbearable
Passion:	Zeal or enthusiasm
Playground:	Park or playing field
Practice:	Do, perform or live out
Questioning:	Inquiring or asking
Quietly:	Silently or calmly
Recognize:	Know or identify
Scared:	Afraid, fearful or nervous
Strike:	Hit, beat or smack
Target:	Aim
Taught:	Past tense of teach
Terrible:	Very bad, appalling or awful
Vigilant:	Cautious
Whether:	Expressing choice or doubt

Printed in the United States
By Bookmasters